just as it was

© Copyright for these poems remains with Pat Taylor.
First published December 2005 by shalom house poetry,
31 The Cairn, Newtownabbey, County Antrim, BT36 6YF.

ISBN: 0-9551896-0-8
       978-0-9551896-0-9

No part of this book may be reproduced or transmitted in any form or by any means without written permission from the publisher, except by a reviewer who wishes to quote brief passages in connection with a review written for insertion in a newspaper, magazine or broadcast. All information contained within the book is correct at the time of going to print.

Printed by Summit Printing
137 Gregg Street, Lisburn bt27 5aw
Tel: 028 9266 5038   Fax: 028 9266 1471
Email: info@summitprinting.co.uk

The cover was designed by Michelle Taylor and the original photographs were taken by John Edwards Walsh, John McClean and David Mayrs.

This book has been funded through the support of the 'Awards for All' scheme.

just as it was

To Helen with best wishes
Pat Taylor

pat taylor

Shalom House Poetry

Acknowledgments

The Shalom House poetry group gratefully acknowledges the 'Awards for All' scheme for its generous funding and support of this publication.

Thanks are due to the Belfast Institute of Further and Higher Education (BIFHE) and the Shalom House Centre, Cliftonville Road, Belfast.

Particular thanks are also due to Moyra Donaldson for her assessment and editing of this collection through the Creative Writers Network poetry programme.

Some of the poems featured in this anthology have been previously published in *Gown*, *The Honest Ulsterman*, *Alchemy* (Creative Writers Network, 2002)) and a number of publications produced by the New Belfast Creative Arts Initiative (NBCAI), including *The Lonely Poet's Guide to Belfast* (2003), *Ringing the Changes* (2004) and *BT1, The Poet's Code* (2005). A selection of Pat's poems also appears in *'Keeping The Colours New'*, an anthology of poems by Shalom House poetry group, published in 2003.

The poem 'And so on' was one of a number of poems engraved on a glass sculpture as one of NBCAI's community poetry programmes. The poem 'Bereft' helped to inspire the design of a memorial window in Belfast City Hall, by the Newtownards artist, Nora Gaston.

Pat Taylor (neé Walsh) was born in Belfast in 1932 and spent her initial childhood years in the city before moving to Claudy, County Derry in 1941. She then returned to the city in 1951 where as a young woman she attended Belfast College of Art, studying under the noted artist John Luke. She married Robert Taylor in 1958 and has 3 children and 6 grandchildren.

Contents

Wake Me	11
34 Brookvale Avenue	12
Rock-A-Bye Tick Tock	13
As Soon As Said	14
Ruined	15
Taking The Cures	16
How To Lose Your Best Friend and Ruin Your Fifth Birthday	17
Four Poems For Bogey From Bacall – 1	18
Impromptu	19
Just As It Was	20
Primitive Pleasures	21
By The River	22
Outside Amenities	23
The Prize	24
The Record Breaker	25
Untouchable	26
Turning Back	27
The Pig And I	28
On The Brink	30
The Priest	31
Hybrids	32
Full Of Nonsense	33
B For Posture	34
Darkey	36
Accumulated Quarts	38
Four Poems For Bogey From Bacall – 2	39
Calf Love	40
Where The Cromlech Stands	41
Legless in Antrim	42
Donald	43
Revelations	44
How I Wish	45
Papa	46
Counted	47

On Being Shallow	48
Too Late	49
That Boyo	50
The Last Enemy	51
Residue	52
Clinging	53
A Time A Place	54
Echoes	56
Keeping Faith	57
Ties	58
Flowering Cherry	59
Just What I Needed	60
By Any Other Name	61
Monday Morning	62
Fettered	64
Away And Back	65
Past And Present	66
My Old Home	67
A Long Stretch Of Imagination	68
Something	69
Return To Learmount	70
Sex Education	72
Above All Else	73
A Growing Silence	74
Four Poems For Bogey From Bacall – 3	75
Four Poems For Bogey From Bacall – 4	77
Organ Retention	78
Bereft	79
Well Round The Corner	80
Old Flame	81
Will You?	82
Redheads At Sunrise	83
Old Photo	84
Gran's Mother	85
Afterlife	86
And So On	87

for my children – David, Felicity and Ross

and my grandchildren – Andrew, Ashleigh and Adam Taylor
and Taylor, Reilly and Flynn Dennison.

WAKE ME

A December blossoming,
these poems.
Thoughts that will remain
when I am gone.

But they will sleep
until this book is read.
So wake me,
let me speak.

34 BROOKVALE AVENUE
1935

Sparkling grains in yellow sandstone,
frilly socks, white patent ankle-ties,
the hem of a flower-patterned dress.
A three-year old pavement artist,
I hunkered, knees hugging my face.

Sun and chubby fingers,
warmed wax crayons,
a present for my birthday.
Breathing their oily odour
I drew fat orange cats
with long purple whiskers.

Crab-apple confetti dappled
Mother and Gran, as they basked
on the blue garden seat.
A sponge, I soaked up colours
scents and scenes.
New ; content ; unsuspecting.

ROCK-A-BYE TICK-TOCK

Bowed wood
rocked
on terra-cotta.
Gran held me safe
hummed
the Merry Widow Waltz,
the turf fire glowed.

A brass moon swung
behind bevelled glass,
the old friend
that eased me into sleep
with tick-tock lullaby.

Heartbeats
Gran's and mine –

AS SOON AS SAID

for David

On the mantelpiece
sepia tinted ghosts:
my father's friends
'still wet behind the ears'
mowed down
in the Somme's red mud –

and round-eyed cousins,
just little girls,
'darling buds', Gran called them –
like the greenhorn soldiers
no inkling of what lay in wait.

I gazed at them each day,
mourned their lives unlived
feared to have tomorrow
savagely snatched away.
Sometimes I'd look in the mirror
and say, "This is me,
I am here, this is now."
But 'now' was always gone
as soon as said.

RUINED

Logs blazed and fissled,
the velvet throat inhaled
exploding stars.
With heated cheeks I sat cross-legged
at Father's tartan feet.
Our rug was reseda green,
thick, hand-knotted by Mother;
she was making another,
measuring and cutting
against a grooved rule.

A standard lamp with long silk fringe
encircled us in amber light,
cast moving pictures on the wall;
rabbits and birds, Father showed me how.
With pearl-trimmed knife
he peeled an apple
all in one wiggley spiral.
As it dropped the fire spat,
showed me a snake.

Then Mother noticed my new doll –
I'd given her a bob,
 'Smarter than ringlets', I thought,
but she cried, "Ruined",
held me back while it burned.
The black throat roared along with mine.

TAKING THE CURES

It's Friday
nose held in a pinch
castor oil poured in
the moment I gasp.

For the sake of clear airways
I'm dragged out to roadworks,
to breathe tar fumes and shame
for ten minute stretches.

Paid sixpence for his trouble,
the rag man takes and shoves me
three times under his stinky old donkey.
I whoop and cough like never before.

When I hear Tom Brown
has been cured by his gran,
(cake made with urine)
I blatter their knocker, beg
her not to go telling my mother.

HOW TO LOSE YOUR BEST FRIEND AND RUIN YOUR FIFTH BIRTHDAY

I need red party shoes,
red *patent* party shoes,
big floppy bows made of satin,
and my hair wound in rags
to make fat bouncy ringlets –
so gorgeous for tossing.

I want some of the things
that lucky Anne White gets
without even asking.
My mother keeps scoffing.
"Only back street girls
are got up like that".
From the vinegar voice
I know it is hopeless.

Needing to hurt,
I blurt this to Ann
who carries it home –
what a disaster!
My mother does her 'don't care' shrug,
"Wee blabber-mouth!" she mutters.

FOUR POEMS FOR BOGEY WITH LOVE FROM BACALL

I - THE PIERCING
1940

I told Vincent we were going
to Claudy for ten whole years –
Halfway up our stairs
he asked my father
for my hand in marriage.
Daddy, po-faced answered,
"You're more than welcome to her."

Betrayal added to my rage.

Outside I pinned the culprit
tight against a climbing rose,
with rigid fingers
drummed him in the chest.
"You're two months younger,"
I snarled, "*and* I'm taller."

He stumbled away, head bowed –
and then I saw that thorns
had pierced the eczema
behind his knees.

IMPROMPTU
Claudy, Co.Derry, 1941

They hated the accent,
the frilly dress, hair
that didn't need hot tongs.
Uprooted from a town,
I'd been shunned
for many's the long day.
From the iron barred windows
of the Bank House
I watched the village children
flay a rubber tyre with sticks.

In our yard an upturned barrow.
Kneeling, I spun the wheel
and taking a scrap end of brass
cut for new stairs,
applied it delicately.
Metal music from whirling spokes –
wind chimes,
rain on deep sea,
the echoing of drowned bells –

I sang me an out of tune song.

JUST AS IT WAS

The sun slanted through
the partly-open gateway
of the old walled-in garden,
an oblique bright rectangle
on the rough stone wall beyond.
With the rattley push-mower
my father sheared
our patch of daisied grass.
By the sun-blistered scullery door
my mother paused,
arms floured to the elbows
and wearing a bleached sack-apron.
She watched as I wheeled our cat
in the old Tansad.

Suddenly still, I looked, listened,
breathing heady scent
of yellow Honeysuckle-azalea
and warm damp new-mown grass;
sensing a need to remember
that moment, just as it was.

PRIMITIVE PLEASURES

Back bowed, boots squarely planted,
skirts and aprons hitched,
thighs spread, devouring heat.

From previous indulging
her shins are mottled,
yellowed, browned, vermilioned.

Elbows on knees, hands rise
to pleasure plough-scarred palms,
sink to give their backs a toasting.

Bloated with porridge,
heavy-lidded, she is lulled
by downdraughts of turf smoke.

Shadows finger the underside of thatch.
Hearth-bound, in a maze of cracks,
the crickets sing.

BY THE RIVER

Lying beside the slow Faughan,
I breathe pungent scent
of warm damp earth.
Dragonflies swoop
above the amber flow.
Fish are hunting too,
there goes the *plump plop*
of a salmon re-entering water
and from a far field, like an echo
the lazy note of ball on willow.

Drifting waist deep
in meadow grasses,
I watch bees fumble busily,
their weight dipping the blooms.
Butterflies rise before me
colours flashing in the sun –
I hear, but do not see
a rabbit drum his warning code.
Entering the cool Plantin
I drink from a spring
that has already spoiled me
for any other water.

OUTSIDE AMENITIES

At Killaloo School
the privies were cleared out
every three months or so.
We cheered the valiant lads
who came with cart and shovels.

Within each wooden stall
a circle cut in planking,
the waste amassing
on cement five feet below.
Looped on rusty nails, hairy cord
threaded newspaper squares.
Ink tattooed both skin and bloomers.

In summer, sometimes retching,
only the desperate ventured,
for dozens of insects
would jostle busily to perch
on helpless backsides.
Lusting for tender pink,
clegs from nearby beasts
sank their vampire teeth.

Once Scotchie, the evacuee,
was caught peeing
into brambles at the back.
With arm twisted up behind,
the Master marched him
to his lair,
breeches yanked to ankles
he was beaten till he bled.

THE PRIZE

My prize at the Church bazaar
in a sack, legs strapped tight.
Cut free, he couldn't stand.
I rubbed the poor cramped feet.

Feathered in glossy burnt sienna
his fluffy bloomers bunched above
smart lizard patterned leggings.
A meaty comb flopped rakishly
shading one eye, then the other.

Flamboyant posturings punctuated
elongated glides with slow unfurling toes.
Each morning boastful cockle-doodlings
soared full throttle, then ricocheting back
rude answers urged him on to bold reply.

My mother soon grew tired of that
and snow spots in the yard.
"He needs hens, not little girls," she said.
I tried so hard, but farms don't keep two cocks.
Then Mother said she'd had success.

On Sunday we had chicken dinner,
the breast so plump, so white, so moist . . . . .

THE RECORD BREAKER

Raired on mushrooms
nettles and snared rabbit,
a skinny-ma-link
with bealin' ears,
her tapeworm
near as desperate as herself.

The mother had no crockery,
no knives, no forks,
an earthen floor her table.
The pan scraped out
Celine and the wee lads
scrimmaged like dogs.

She held the record –
the only child at Killaloo
who'd never missed a day.
Glowing she'd fairly swell
when this was marvelled on.

But the Master turfed her out
for turning up with spots
that shouted Chicken Pox.
The most enormous tears
we ever saw
splashed to the floor.

Hell-bent to keep her precious record
she'd do the three mile trek,
but everyday sent back.
No kindness of free milk.
No present mark.

UNTOUCHABLE

Molly and Isabel, both thirteen,
were set apart from us.
Nits beaded greasy hair,
mature insects manoeuvred
from strand to strand.

Ragged garments
fairly reeked after a soaking
on the long trudge to school.
Isabel was barefoot
and on Molly's boots
loose steel shod tips and heels
clacked like castanets.

At lunch hour
we chanted rhymes
for skipping games
and bulgy-cheeked, ate greedily
from well-stocked paper bags.
They never spoke to us
nor even to each other, just stood
by the playground wall.

Smiling, tongue-tied,
I offered sandwiches
gingerly and at arms-length.
Unmoving, they stared,
stony-faced.
I turned away, ten years old,
defeated, not understanding.

Maybe in later years
they had a better life.
Someone must know.
I want a happy ending.

TURNING BACK

After the fair
an ancient dog lay on
hitched to a water pump.
A sorry sight, dejected,
hobbled with rheumatic pain.
dreadlocks dangling
from his rancid coat.

The owner, sozzled, carted off,
the old sheepdog forgotten.
I trailed it home
fearing Mother's wrath,
but drooping stance
and clouded lenses
touched her hard-boiled heart.

We donned gas masks,
rubber gloved
cut off the tangles.
Four whole weeks
we groomed and bathed,
fed him well.
But still depressed
with wilting head
his gait was stiff and slow.

Next fair day the farmer came.
A miracle! An instant pup
cavorting friskily around!
The bent old man
astride his bike began to pedal,
the dog to run, but turning back
he came to lick my mother's hand.

THE PIG AND I

All through summer
I helped Theresa feed
the pig kept shut
in a rickety shed.
Dazzled by sudden light,
he would blink through
lush pink lashes,
as we lowered
the scrap-laden bucket
over the half door.

Each week his snout
became much easier to pet,
for the pile of filth
and straw he stood on
grew in height.

Theresa, farm-hardened,
laughed when I murmured,
"What a lovely boy!"
I begged to take him for a walk,
fed him apples and bananas
Mother thought *I* ate
and later shared a birthday cake.

The day the killer came
they said, "Away on off now."
But peering round the gable
I saw the first abortive blow.

Searing soprano
chased my fleeing heels
as I went rushing up one street
and down the other
through our house
and up the stairs
blown by a storm.

That evening I found him,
scoured clean, upside down,
skewered in obscene arabesque.
His middle open, empty,
innards glistening
heaped and spilling
over the sides
of a rusty barrow.
From under pink silk lashes
gazed irises of stone.

Theresa tapped my shoulder,
handed me a basin, said,
"Here's kidneys for your mother."

ON THE BRINK

Roots are bared
by the eroding flow,
bleached by July's sun.
The willow leans
over deep water
fingering a drowned image.
The air is so still
and yet the tree trembles –
fish flirt
among her summer leaves.

THE PRIEST

i.m. Fr James Quinn, 1930-2005

James Quinn aged twelve
behind the counter of the family store,
eyes dark - the centres of pansies,
skin to suit Miss Pears.

I even loved the cut of him –
rainbow jumper with puffed sleeves-
and the steps 'n' stairs siblings
arrayed in scrap wool (his war effort)
'One pattern, one size does rightly' –
a change from socks for soldiers.

In a wee house out the back,
a gutted Austin 12, James learned to cook,
dosed me with cabbage, then custard,
whiff of sty and hen-run all around.

Turned sixteen, caring for the poor,
he made them soups, baked soda bread –
but driven by his father's cane
was collared for the Holy life
that locks away young men in prayer -
broke the hearts of all us girls.

*   *   *

Frail and elderly James limped home
free at last to answer his calling.
Creeds unheeded, he cared for those in need,
made soup, baked soda bread.

HYBRIDS

Theresa and her brothers
came to our Orange Hall,
blew wetly into unresponsive flutes,
whanged the Lambeg drum.
They took me up the brae
to band practice at St.Patrick's,
showed me Irish dance steps
and we leaped and stomped
to the National beat.
On banner-swinging days
we pranced beside
whatever band was on the go
and cheered our marching friends.

One Fair day, chomping Yellow Man,
we bought with our last pennies
brightly coloured Sacred Hearts,
embroidered, made of felt
they had secret bits inside.
Happy with these treasures,
we pinned them to our woolly vests.
At bed time I was puzzled,
wondered why my mother giggled.

FULL OF NONSENSE

Learmount Castle

A bank of rhodendrons
sloped steeply to the river.
Above, Learmount
reared against the sky.
Gargoyles snarled at us
and from the portico
speared dragons glared
across the woods.

There were no private moments
at boarding school,
so I'd excuse myself from class
and dashing up the servants' stairs
would pace the main landing,
imaginary fan clicking and rippling.

Reaching the grand staircase,
I'd sweep back my long hair,
head high, descending,
one hand languidly trailing mahogany,
the other raising the hem
of my flowing gown.

Stepping delicately across
checkerboard marble
I'd pause graciously,
as the Prince bowed low.

I'd lose all sense of time:
only clanging brass
would return me to the reality
of gym slip, ink-stained fingers
and the cold spaces
between stockings and interlock knickers.

B FOR POSTURE

We'd groan as Matron
crossed the dorm,
heels hammering
the polished floor.
"Hup now gels," she'd say
and brass rings
would scrape and clatter
as curtains jerked
to show us coal-black sky.

Filled the night before
papier-mâché basins
waited in a row.
The prefects on duty
smashed the ice
and stayed to make certain
we stripped to our waists
and shocked all our bits.

They had the power to bestow
big and little B's and G's,
the totals each month
revealed at assembly.
No matter how I tried
I couldn't get a G of any size,
the B's flowed thick and fast,
all given for bad posture
I couldn't seem to fix.

At every mealtime
they'd stick pins in me
and I was warned
if I didn't straighten soon,
I'd walk the length
of the common room, nude,
a book on my head
and all the prefects watching.

The term before I came
a girl leaped from a window.
I was sad for her, quite certain
she had suffered from bad posture.

DARKEY

The Yankee soldiers left behind
a crossbred cocker pup.
Smiley-eyed his thumping tail
shimmied every inch of body.
I couldn't have a pet,
he found a home next door.

It was me he loved the best.
We roamed the countryside.
I saved scraps, stole extras,
made a secret bed.

One day a rumour speared me.
I collared Mrs. Boyle.
"Aye that's so," she said.
"What's more, Tom bungled it.
Them stones was far too light…
he had a quare slow death.
*But you're the one's to blame,
you should'a' let the wee dog be."*

I found the sack in the Faughan,
caught beneath the old Red Bridge.
Head above water,
lifted to the sky,
wet weave traced
his eyes, his muzzle,
paws were raised as if he begged.

Mother said I'd made Boyle jealous,
to covet and entice was wrong.

Five years on, deserted and morose,
he hanged himself, another bungling,
one boot in touch with earth –
a quare slow death.

Still mourning, I did not care.

ACCUMULATED QUARTS

Stone-floored, the waiting room,
grand for muck-caked boots
and projectile tobacco juice
that missed the spittoon (mostly
their aim was just astounding).
Through sickly-sweetish pipe-fug
I saw each seasoned farmer
a bottle jutting from his pocket.
Some swathed in newsprint,
those without gleamed amber,
each a *quart* of sample for the doctor.

One old man nursed two,
perhaps delivering for the missus.
By the look of things,
wives had no time to run to doctors.
Spoiled by city comforts I sat stiffly,
skirts safely gathered in,
thought myself among tramps;
didn't recognise moneyed men
right under my nose.

FOUR POEMS FOR BOGEY WITH LOVE FROM BACALL

II - ME AND THE DUTCH REFUGEE
Belfast revisited, 1944

We queue in the last hour
of grubby light – share sweetie cigs.
I watch my breath curl.
I'm doing Bacall,
hair veiling one cheek.
Vincent is Bogey – collar up,
smile crooked, because of his ciggy.

Chips cost us sixpence,
we head for a waterworks bench,
delve into newspaper layers.
Bogey is sniffing –
his specks stream over,
I think of the Bisto Kids Poster.

Still on the hot side
each chip gets a wave in raw air.
(The swans get excited)
With quick swigs of Ross's
we manage to munch.

A tram in the distance
is girning and clanking.
We'll need to hop on
to be home before blackout.

CALF LOVE

Wherever he went,
there I was;
secretly worshipping:
at cricket matches
tennis, badminton.
It began when I was twelve,
straddled on our school wall.
He rode the lane on a red tractor,
knight on charger.
It was those eyes
that claimed me,
eyes like blue fire
that flashed their smile
in my direction.

No matter what age I became
I was always ten years younger.
He liked me that's for sure,
sought me out at fifteen,
applied my first kiss.
Twice a week we spooned
in the Church hall basement.
But it was a more
sophisticated girl he 'went with'.
Such a mistake I made
bringing her to badminton.

WHERE THE CROMLECH STANDS

Nothing but shadows
beyond the sun-freckled hollow,
ferns hem the legacy of stone.

Brambles weave in the hawthorn,
blood-seeping fruit
long gone,
only lusty barbs
promise a spring blossoming.
Strung between the ancient rocks
a spider's snare,
polka-dot flies
appliquéd in silk.

A rush of air
sets patterns shimmying
across the ground.
High above, oak leaves
spiral and rise –
a cloud
of migrating butterflies.

LEGLESS IN ANTRIM

Bertie was legless,
not due to drink, but smokes.
"Auld veins cannae thole them."
Clamped in a wheelchair
he minded the shop,
a bottle parked beneath the counter
for when he'd need to pee.

Tipped off, the local peelers
on the hunt for poteen, barged inside
and pounced on Bertie's bottle.
In cracker form,
the Sergeant raised it to his lips –
downed a right auld swig.

DONALD

Cracked nails and calluses
could not disguise well-knit fingers
as they raced across ivory.
The old man swayed, fanning leather pleats.
Mud-caked boot stamped out the beat,
metal rang on stone.
He knew many's the auld come-all-ye,
his country twang enhanced each tune.

The peelers were never done
trying to find red diesel in his motor
or poteen stashed away.
They searched the farmhouse,
chimneys, hedges, muckheaps,
with spiteful regularity.

And so, a mere three months apart,
Donald drove across two sets of polished toes,
on point duty in Antrim.

Feeling his ninety years, he saw the ad.,
'Domestos kills all known germs dead'
and then began to dose himself.
There was no stopping him.
Supplies were dotted all around
but these were just red herrings,
others, as slyly tucked away as poteen,
only came to light long after.

REVELATIONS

The undertaker helped me make my bed.
I was tickled. "Unusual this," I thought,
"few could boast of such a thing."
A patient at the Royal, like myself,
he'd sauntered down the ward to flirt.
Odd, the subject chosen to accompany the 'glad eye'.
He related how corpses were stood in a row,
tilted, weight on heads and heels, hosed down.

In busy February they'd be stacked like cards,
no class or sex discrimination,
willy-nilly, ladies, tramps, names tagged.
His workmates disrespectful,
stumped out cigarettes on boobs and other bits,
made lewd remarks, crude jokes.
Crisp packets, coke bottles, junk of any kind
got dumped in caskets ordered to be sealed.
(To flabbergast some future archaeologist?)

I know a lovely lady who goes to homes
to lay out Jewish women,
maybe she'll oblige her Gentile neighbour.

HOW I WISH

I

They yanked the covers down,
stripped the Victorian body,
pillaged further with catheter and drip,
without a second glance
or kindly word, moved on.

II

Gran confined by metal bars
robbed of flannel nightdress,
familiar Woolsey vests, her cardigan.
Head bowed to hear the tale
I warm her hand against my cheek.

Pleading doesn't bring results,
no blankets can be had,
the store is locked until the morning.
Gran's things are not permitted.
The white-starched Sister
will not give one blanket
from an empty bed.

III

How I wish I'd stood my ground,
said I'd phone the local papers,
send for Ian Paisley,
anything it took –
but I gave in,
let the bully crush me.

On the death certificate
no mention of Hypothermia.

PAPA

i.m. John Edwards Walsh, 1888-1973

My father hoed happily among azaleas.
Late March sun warmed moist earth
and teasing spring scents rose.
Daffodil shoots jostled eagerly,
thrusting upwards, measuring time.

He was eighty-four and stooped,
the legacy of trench warfare
and two bullets still present,
pleasant face seemed so young to me.

I approached with toddling son
across the lawn.
Rather deaf, he missed our greeting,
but caught sight of movement.
"Ah there you are!" he beamed, turning,
"There you are and there's that fine big boy!
What do you think of the garden, Patsy?"

II

A diamond day for the funeral.
Birds send love notes tree to tree,
daffodils now in bloom, dip as we pass.
Half my roots gone, I promise to care for his garden.

COUNTED

Almost hidden
by fallen leaves,
feathers crinolined,
beak dipped in speckled ruff.

Thistledown in cradling hands,
laboured breathing presses sharp bone
against my fingers.

ON BEING SHALLOW

My father loved H.P.
Applied it lavishly
to stews and fries and grills.

At my wedding,
he surpassed himself.
Hearty clouts
splurged sauce in soup.

Shocked, I shrank
a good two inches.
The social error huge,
a dark cloud, unforgettable.

He died when Ross was three.
Small matter then
where sauce should go
or who might see.

If I just had another chance,
"Look," I'd shout. "We love H.P.",
and I would douse my soup
to keep my father company.

TOO LATE

All those years –
sea and land between.

I am the girl I was then –
the woman I am now.

And you,
the boy, the man

looking at me
the way you did before.

What if?
The thought is pushed away.

You bolder –
ask me where and when.

THAT BOYO…

…outwitting me for fifteen years,
sneaking back inside
when newly ejected,
streaking unheeding
to hide upstairs –
curlicued in the airing-press,
vibrating like a motor mower
among inherited linens.

There wasn't a door
or drawer that foxed him,
the fridge was raided, meat hooked,
eggshells scattered on the tiles.
Our relentless killing machine,
decorated the doormat
with saliva-soaked birds.
We screamed abuse
and whacked, so he
took to hiding them
under the azaleas.

He was some cute boyo,
him and his party tricks –
charming his way back into my arms,
patting my cheek with velvet mitt.
When I went walking
he'd trot parallel
through all the gardens,
constantly in touch
with catty chit-chat.

THE LAST ENEMY

i.m. Robert Jamison Taylor, 1934-1984

At the first sign of a cold
he was away off to bed
with chocolates, booze,
a war story and the T.V.
"Do a roast of lamb," he'd say,
in the same breath
as telling me how ill he felt.

When we heard *that word*
there were seven days left.
He asked nothing from me,
hid the pain that drew sweat,
but never a tear,
sealed me off,
did not share his dying.

Dazed, no words of comfort
passed my lips.

RESIDUE

Funny some of the things
tucked away in your wallet.
A faded picture –
I was just sixteen.
The Catholic 'keep me safe'
and you a 'Right Footed' cop!
An ancient ticket
for a Nashville show.

The good things went
quite some time ago.
I gave our eldest
your heavy fishing coat,
the Omega watch,
a splendid evening suit.

Your sister simply
chose a single tie,
but I sent a locket
with a twist of hair inside;
cut while you lay
in the sinister polished box.

I'll keep these old cords.
Do you remember me
teasing in the car?
I stroked your knee and swore
velvet turned me on.
You pretended panic, said,
"People on the bus will see!"
How we laughed, two months ago.

CLINGING

For a while when I opened the wardrobe
I would breathe the remembered scent,
clean-soaped skin, Old Spice, tobacco.
Sometimes I'd creep inside and, closing the door,
would savour you all around me.

The scent is gone now, the clothes musty.
Inside your shoes my hands find
the shape of your feet, deeply imprinted.

There is a corner of this room
where you would tap and blow the shaver clear;
I used to watch with silent disapproval –

Here in the dust, I know traces of you remain.

A TIME, A PLACE

It's been six months
and I've not parted
with a single tear.
They battle to surface
when friends murmur
their notions of comfort,
or at family moments,
no longer shared.

In the supermarket,
still programmed I reach
for your favourite.
I abandon the trolley
and tears on tight rein
dash homewards,
mad for the relief
of letting go.
But here I am again.
with desert eyes.

I'm tired of labouring on,
being strong for everyone,
dishing out help and comfort
as regularly as meals.

In the empty house
I wallow in bath water
and self-pity.
'How could you?
Dying like that….
Leaving me to cope!'
Crying at last
I howl my rage
volume up full blast.

Spent, throat aching,
I pull on a robe
to answer relentless rat-a-tats.
The police are here,
"A neighbour was concerned."

ECHOES

Around six, headlights
would swing through the gates.
I'd hear the staccato pings
of metal on ceramic,
the thud of heavy oak,
a cheerful booming
greeting our kids in the hall;
then a great bear hug for me
by the kitchen sink.

He was big and loud
very good and very bad.

Now he neither comes nor goes –
ash rests in a metal urn
and the empty days and nights
yawn endlessly ahead.

I exist with echoes
filtering from one room to another.

KEEPING FAITH

A crisp, bright day, late in September,
we sit on the steps and plan
how the garden will be next summer.
Steam curls from our mugs, dampening faces,
we cradle the heat in welcoming hands.

Only a few weeks later, I lift the polished lid,
take the wedding ring from my finger,
slip it under your palm –

A summer's day,
a sense of presence brings me peace.
I don't regret my ruined hands,
my aching back, my wounded knee –
this is the garden we planned.

TIES

The beach is empty –

a vast expanse of sea
and sand and sky.

I sift ecru grains
through fingers that are young
and know this is a dream –

like the one of you, so real,
touching your face, feeling stubble.

Waking in pallid light
one of your ties has inched
beneath the wardrobe door –

I've kept them all these years.

FLOWERING CHERRY

i.m. Gillian Turney, died aged nineteen

I was used to Airport red tape
and petty spitefulness of searchers,
but this . . . .
"A wheelchair will not be provided,
security reasons, Madam."

Struggling with tears,
I put our cases on a trolley,
drape the tired girl on the top.
She tells me not to worry,
swears the ride is cool.

So typical of Gill.
At home, to spare her parents,
she plays the game,
'Getting Better-Doing Well,'

but me, she asks
to plant a flowering cherry
to remember her by.

JUST WHAT I NEEDED

i.m. Vida Caroline Walsh, 1896 – 1987

At fifty four my hands
were already ruined,
so her rings and bracelets
I gave to my daughter –
wonderful on young skin.

Some clothes
went to the Sally Army,
the most expensive
to elderly cousins.
I kept nothing,
a mistake to be hasty
in shock and sorrow.

Months passed
before I cleared the floor
of the built-in cupboard.
There it lay,
her bowling anorak,
lightweight, warm, bright yellow.
I slipped it on –
a sunny hug from Mother.

BY ANY OTHER NAME

Vida was her name,
the feminine of David,
but it never crossed his lips, not ever.
Dad wrote letters that began,
'My dearest girl',
but as soon as they were wed
he called her 'Mam'.
I was born and she became
forever afterwards, 'The Mammy'.
Now too late to ask,
I'm curious and wonder
why he could not speak her name.

MONDAY MORNING

Claudy 31st July 1972

The village wallows in July sunshine.
In the middle of the road
auld Divin's dog lies snoring,
the few cars trickling through
carefully avoiding him.

It's too early for corner boys
to be lounging at the crossroads,
but Liz Mc Elhinney,
twenty years engaged, newly wed,
leans by the door of her husband's pub,
watches Willie Temple deliver milk.
Sixteen years ago she delivered him,
now on his first day at work,
he stops whistling to grin and wave.

Labourers arrive to dig a trench,
brawny, bronzed, all local talent;
an assortment of folk gather
to await the Derry bus.

Across the street,
Kathryn cleans a corner window,
poised on sill, tiptoes to reach.
Inside his shop, her Granda raises a Coke
in promise and approval.
Dimples show - and then she's gone.

A wave of shards and milk
and Willie's done for.

Liz Mc Elhinney is on fire.

On down the road....
a safety pin in dungarees
may help to tell the name.

FETTERED

for Ross

His ink-soiled hand is cramped,
bored; he hates the endless notes.
Penned by the desk, his colt legs
impatient for release,
last few months at school,
gear, shabby and frayed
made to do.

Sparsely-padded bones
are punished by the bench.
On the pale clock-face,
a trailing hand
still forty minutes lacking.

His old Swan falters,
the tedious chant
a soup of ancient alphabets.

Sunlight sidles through summer leaves
and patterns the scuff-marked floor.

He skives behind those languid lids.

AWAY AND BACK

I saw they didn't feel like me,
the girls I'd grown up with
since the age of nine,
they were not sad
that I was leaving.
Perhaps I'd never fitted in,
town to country isn't easy.

I wandered round my empty home
with words I could not say aloud.
(Not a good thing
to be heard talking to a house.)
I'm smiling now to think of it –
I'd talked to my old haunts,
promised to come back to them,
fiercely etched their beauty on my eye.

All of forty years went past
before I managed to return.
Driving across the mountain
at reckless speed, I was crazy to arrive,
believing all would be the same.

PAST AND PRESENT

The first thing
is the lack of trees.
Even the ancient oaks
that once encircled the Stone Age Fort
are sorry stumps.

A shirt factory has arisen
from the old slate quarry.
We sailed home-made boats here,
teased the pond-skaters,
gathered frog spawn to hatch at home.
The cool green Plantin
bluebells stream and spring
inviolate,
interned by council housing.

The cricket field's built over.
Rugged Balnamean Bridge
cemented, streamlined.
Wild strawberries will not inhabit these walls,
and nowadays, no dog would dare
to snooze in the middle of the road.

Before me the plough-raped meadow.
Wooden stakes and barbed wire
imprison the Faughan.
I stumble alongside
heading for the Boat Hole
where we learned to swim.

Not a dragonfly in sight,
not a leaping fish.

The river has become shallow.

MY OLD HOME

The house is empty,
paint peeling,
windows dulled by grime.
The door to the walled-in garden
groans on sagging hinges –
all is rank and tangled,
crows, startled and indignant
flap heavily away.

I stood here long ago,
tried to hold a moment close,
imprisoned and secure.

A LONG STRETCH OF IMAGINATION

Since childhood I have walked here;
the seasons change, but little else.

In sensible shoes,
warm ribbed tights, tweed skirt,
my hands –
the crimpled skin of crêpe de Chine.

Saffron, tangerine and burnt sienna,
luscious drifts, whispery-crisp –
no one to see me toe-up leaves.

Red patent ankle-ties,
polka-dot socks,
firm golden limbs.

My frilly dress is robe-of-voile,
I'm almost skipping now,
going to a party.

SOMETHING

From deep grasses
serpentine arms entreat –
a fallen angel, ashen faced,
tracks of sooty tears.

Porcelain doves peep
through lichen-clouded domes.

The family headstone
delayed in mid-descent.
My fingers trace blurred words.

Massive yews loom in fading light,
statues cluster, heads tilted,
under hooded lids, stone cataracts.

Moss swallows my footsteps.
Need to be gone,
fast as in that dream
where something follows.

RETURN TO LEARMOUNT

for Mina McClean

One of the dragons
is missing from the portico
and the eyes of the Castle
are blanked by hardboard.
Vandals have bludgeoned a hole
through the breeze-blocked doorway.

Anna won't entertain it.
She wrings her hands,
says tramps or worse
might be lurking.
She's going back
to sit in the car,
with all the doors locked.

But neither fear nor age
can curb me,
I wriggle through the gap.
Stench of decay.
My torch shows the Adam ceiling –
its clusters of oak leaves.

Darkness yawns
on each side:
I am stilled
on black and white marble.

Lost in shadows
I see the children
we had been,
hear the tap and scuffle
of many indoor shoes
on polished wood.

Fallen plaster, rubble, rubbish
At last some light.
A grimy jewelled glow
arching above the stairway.
We sang carols here,
six little girls to each rise
stained glass behind us.

The mahogany treads seem sound.
Up, up and around I go.
My dorm.
A brass 2 still on the door.
Water has run down walls,
the decomposing floor sags.
Lit by my unsteady beam
clumps of dark fungi quiver and rear.
"Buildings are like people," I think,
"better remembered as they were."

SEX EDUCATION

Oh boy how times have changed!
At the age of twelve, four of us,
including Sergeant Plunkett's daughter,
locked ourselves in the lavatory
at the village Police Station.

Naughtily excited, we looked up 'piss'
in Nuttal's Standard Dictionary.
What a crashing disappointment 'urine' proved to be.
I can't think what we had expected.

Angel, the minister's youngest had a cunning plan
and so we searched for 'cock'.

*'Male bird, familiar form of address,
to place a hat on the side of the head'*,

left us stumped, but not for long.

We knew a woman's 'thingy'
was often called a 'teapot' and tried that next.
'Vessel with a spout', we thought
much more suitable for 'cock'
and laughed ourselves silly.

ABOVE ALL ELSE

I know this scent.
It hints of Autumn....
my eyes say Summer.
Swayed in high branches
I am tranquil in the sun.

Beyond auld Divin's meadow,
the lazy Faughan
still amber with flax-soak,
spills at the weir.

Circling the Plantin,
fields roll and swell
like rumpled eiderdowns
of shaded silk.
Far below, flickering shadows
Brindle pine-needled earth.

My bones suggest
a different Autumn
and Winter will follow.

One day, rooted,
I will only stand
and gaze at budding fingers
as they stroke manilla-blue.

A GROWING SILENCE

I used to be afraid
to walk the narrow flower-edged path,
alive with bees and dragonflies
so many criss-crossed busily.

My world back then was full of 'flutter-byes'
that glowed and flashed like neon signs.
At dusk I'd close my windows tight
as bats in droves swooped on furry-bodied moths.
At dawn, birdsong volume up full blast
would slaughter sleep.

Irises, bulrushes, cotton, arms laden
I'd squelch through Brolly's Bog,
hear from fields of swaying gold
the corncrakes relay raucous code.

These days wild bees are few
and my fingers are enough to count
the butterflies this season.
In the garden a solitary bird
spills her summer song.

FOUR POEMS FOR BOGEY WITH LOVE FROM BACALL

III - IN THE ARCHAEOLOGY SECTION
2003

On the cover
a Celtic sea horse.
Author....
'The brilliance of Vincent van Heiff.'
Could it be?

I recall with belated sympathy,
a lonely refugee,
handicapped by ugly specs,
flat feet
and horrid itchy eczema.

Stifling a giggle,
I hear again
impatient tramping
as he took a leak –
(he couldn't bear to miss
a second of our games.)

In those wartime days,
I was the brilliant one
who led him headlong
into every kind of devilment.
His nurse and grandparents
saw me as both godsend and disaster.

Rushing home I scribble
sixty years of news
from No3 and No5,
say I still remember
the picture on the baby-grand –
his beautiful young mother.

A letter rockets back.
'Well, well, well,' it starts –
and at the end, 'My yiddisha mamma
is still alive and ninety-seven.
To be continued.
Bogey.'

FOUR POEMS FOR BOGEY WITH LOVE FROM BACALL

IV - GAME WITHOUT END.
2003

It just struck me.
Bogey's fame could stem
from a game
that I cooked up for Sundays.

We buried notes in jam pots
and little treasures,
mostly other peoples –
his grandma's lorgnette,
his pappa's time piece,
not a sausage from No5 –
no flies on me.
We kept top secret maps
to aid our digging
in the months to follow.

No word of Bogey
from the age of twelve –
he sailed off to Australia.
My years in Claudy
saw me tramping round
old forts and cromlechs,
excavating arrow-heads and axes.

Sixty years on and back in No5,
I watch the digs on Sky,
search antique emporiums
for Celtic artifacts
and end up in the library,
where I find the book
that lets me know
Bogey is still digging.

ORGAN RETENTION

My Father

Revolving metal
bit through flesh and bone,
the spill on stainless steel
slid down the drain.
They helped themselves
to brain and heart –
eleven major organs.

*   *   *

I took scissors
to my hair,
slipped the swirls
beneath your neck,
did not feel the sutures,
did not know
below the shroud
a livid Y evisceration
ran from throat
to pelvic floor.

*   *   *

After thirty years,
a list of what was taken,
a letter saying sorry.

BEREFT

Red ribbons
in the evening sky,
black night
in my heart.
I am a leaf
on a tree,
fingered by the wind
filigreed with frost –
but it is love, love, love,
that I am dying of.

WELL ROUND THE CORNER

Toe nails out of focus,
disobliging knees
and lower back –
scissors will not
reach my feet.
Roles reversed, Ross kneels
to tie my laces.

All the while
the world is mumbling
muscles slacken,
skin seersuckers.
A rhino drip hovers
after soup or curry –

Filled with dread
I exercise my pelvic floor.

OLD FLAME

I enter the ward searching
for jet hair –
a look-alike for Cary Grant.
Four old men
gaze in my direction.
I turn to leave,
one says, "Is that yourself?"

Hair silvered,
face pallid, slack,
eyes cloudy ringed –
but still a glimmer
of the lad remembered.

He seems bemused –
I fancy he's expected
someone willowy, attractive.
I think about the back seat
of a rusty Austin Six,
his tanned face cleanly carved.

Now, taking my hand
he leans feebly to kiss,
I am pretending not to notice
the catheter apparatus.

WILL YOU?

Beside iron pleats
I dream of a turf blaze –
white ash floating,
wafting out across the hearth,
hypnotic scent wending through
every cranny of our home.

My eyes stray to Ben Madigan –
a rash of buildings mars the slopes.
I dream of Sawell and Dart,
their rolling wave, wild and free
where scud clouds chase their shadows.

Who would climb so high for me,
to scatter ash?

REDHEADS AT SUNRISE

I watch
as you part your robe –
the little ones kiss
their unborn brother,
stroke the curve of his cradle.

Framed by the window
three auburn heads
catch the rising sun.

Spellbound,
I gather these moments
for the wintering of months apart.

OLD PHOTO

White Rocks Strand –
you and that smile,
the Wishing Arch.

If I could slip through,
run to you,
bare feet on warm sand.

GRAN'S MOTHER

in loving memory of Emma Ross, 1828 -1900

Gran, youngest of eleven,
said you were a 'wee body'.
Gentle, steel
in plain homespun.
I learned to love you
by her knee.

If ailing, you buried
your hands in earth;
a garden poultice,
to draw out poisons,
give new life.
I laughed at that.

You taught my Gran
unwritten rules
for kindly living.
I keep them yet,
have passed them on intact.

With moments left
you offered comfort.
"Remembered with love
we never truly die."

Kneeling in the garden
I think of you now,
my hands in earth.

AFTERLIFE

for Felicity

Mourning
you turned your eyes
from his image,
closed your lips
on his name.

So many years,
nothing has changed.

Do not shut *me* away,
these poems are my thoughts.

Read me.
Find me. I am in you too.

Wear a red dress,
put on your dancing shoes.

AND SO ON

Do not be sad.
Rather, think of me
as multiplied
and multiplying;
in you and yours
and theirs.